INSPIRATION

summersdale

INSPIRATION

Summersdale Publishers Ltd
46 West Street
Chichester
West Sussex
PO19 1RP
UK

www.summersdale.com

Printed and bound in China

ISBN: 978-1-84953-385-0

Substantial discounts on bulk quantities of Summersdale books are available to corporations, professional associations and other organisations. For details contact Nicky Douglas by telephone: +44 (0) 1243 756902, fax: +44 (0) 1243 786300 or email: nicky@summersdale.com.

To...

From...

Introduction

Inspiration can be rare and elusive, causing frustration for those who wish to harness its power. This book is filled with quotations to motivate and enlighten you, along with mindful tips to help you tap into your own well of inspiration, wherever you are, at any time of day. Enjoy discovering the freedom of a creative and more energetic approach to life.

Know yourself
and you will win
all battles.

Sun Tzu

The greater the
obstacle, the
more glory in
overcoming it.

Molière

Far away there in the sunshine are my highest aspirations. I may not reach them, but I can look up and see their beauty, believe in them, and try to follow where they lead.

Louisa May Alcott

IF WE WAIT FOR THE MOMENT WHEN EVERYTHING, ABSOLUTELY EVERYTHING IS READY, WE SHALL NEVER BEGIN.

Ivan Turgenev

First say to yourself
what you would
be; and then do what
you have to do.

Epictetus

Man's greatness lies in his power of thought.

Blaise Pascal

Join an art class and
see where the muse
leads you.

How wonderful it is that nobody need wait a single moment before starting to improve the world.

Anne Frank

Some run swiftly;
some creep painfully;
all who keep on will
reach the goal.

Piyadassi Thera

FALL SEVEN TIMES, STAND UP EIGHT.

Japanese proverb

Few things are impossible to diligence and skill. Great works are performed not by strength, but perseverance.

Samuel Johnson

A journey of a
thousand miles begins
with a single step.

Lao Tzu

There is no chance,
no destiny,
no fate, that can
hinder or control
the firm resolve of a
determined soul.

Ella Wheeler Wilcox

Have a go on a musical instrument – you may discover a hidden talent.

A man may fulfil the object of his existence by asking a question he cannot answer, and attempting a task he cannot achieve.

Oliver Wendell Holmes

Aim for the moon.
If you miss, you may
hit a star.

W. Clement Stone

THE FUTURE BELONGS TO THOSE WHO BELIEVE IN THE BEAUTY OF THEIR DREAMS.

Eleanor Roosevelt

Life shrinks or
expands in proportion
to one's courage.

Anaïs Nin

A certain amount of opposition is a great help to a man. Kites rise against and not with the wind.

John Neal

Attempt the impossible in order to improve your work.

Bette Davis

*Notice the birds
singing and sit and
listen to them.*

It is right to be
contented with what
we have, but never
with what we are.

James Mackintosh

Never

underestimate the power of passion.

Eve Sawyer

Better than a hundred
years of idleness

Is one day spent in
determination.

Siddhārtha Gautama Buddha

SATISFACTION LIES IN THE EFFORT, NOT IN THE ATTAINMENT. FULL EFFORT IS FULL VICTORY.

Mahatma Gandhi

Life is a progress, and not a station.

Ralph Waldo Emerson

Fear is only as deep
as the mind allows.

Japanese proverb

Go to a live drama or music performance – the experience could blow you away!

There is no impossibility to him who stands prepared to conquer every hazard.

Sarah J. Hale

Only those who
have the patience
to do simple things
perfectly will acquire
the skill to do difficult
things easily.

Friedrich Schiller

The time is
always right to do
what is right.

Martin Luther King Jr

The people who get
on in this world are
the people who get
up and look for the
circumstances they
want, and, if they
can't find them,
make them.

George Bernard Shaw

Regret for wasted time
is more wasted time.

Mason Cooley

DWELL IN POSSIBILITY.

Emily Dickinson

Talents are best
nurtured in solitude,
but character is best
formed in the stormy
billows of the world.

Johann Wolfgang von Goethe

*Take a day out to visit
a city and its churches,
historic buildings and
cultural sites.*

Nothing can stop
the man with the right
mental attitude from
achieving his goal.

Thomas Jefferson

The way to gain a
good reputation is to
endeavour to be what
you desire to appear.

Socrates

All great achievements require time.

Maya Angelou

The only journey is the one within.

Rainer Maria Rilke

Collect as precious pearls the words of the wise and virtuous.

Abd al-Qādir

IF WE ALL DID THE
THINGS WE ARE
CAPABLE OF
DOING, WE WOULD
LITERALLY
ASTOUND OURSELVES.

Thomas A. Edison

*Discover some poetry
you have never read
before and choose
a favourite piece to
commit to heart.*

Exert your talents, and distinguish yourself, and don't think of retiring from the world, until the world will be sorry that you retire.

Samuel Johnson

You must first be who
you really are,
then do what you
need to do, in
order to have what
you want.

Margaret Young

It is hard to fail, but it is worse never to have tried to succeed.

Theodore Roosevelt

Our greatest glory
consists not in never
falling, but in rising
every time we fall.

Oliver Goldsmith

Always be ready to speak your mind, and a base man will avoid you.

William Blake

We must have
perseverance and
above all confidence
in ourselves.

Marie Curie

*There are opportunities
for everything under
the sun out there – go
and find them!*

To be yourself
in a world that is
constantly trying to
make you something
else is the greatest
accomplishment.

Ralph Waldo Emerson

THE WAY TO GET STARTED IS TO QUIT TALKING AND BEGIN DOING.

Walt Disney

Do what you feel
in your heart to be
right – for you'll be
criticised anyway.

Eleanor Roosevelt

Obstacles are those frightful things you see when you take your eyes off the goal.

Henry Ford

Courage is resistance
to fear, mastery of fear
– not absence of fear.

Mark Twain

Small opportunities
are often the beginning
of great enterprises.

Demosthenes

Get chatting to other people and you'll soon be inspired when they reveal their past experiences – perhaps exotic travel, historical events or incidents of bravery.

Life is either a daring adventure or nothing.

Helen Keller

A wise man will make
more opportunities
than he finds.

Francis Bacon

THE QUESTION SHOULD BE, IS IT WORTH TRYING TO DO, NOT CAN IT BE DONE.

Allard K. Lowenstein

Nothing is a waste of time if you use the experience wisely.

Auguste Rodin

When it is obvious
that the goals cannot
be reached, don't
adjust the goals, adjust
the action steps.

Confucius

I see my path, but I don't know where it leads. Not knowing where I'm going is what inspires me to travel it.

Rosalia de Castro

One may walk over
the highest mountain
one step at a time.

John Wanamaker

*Visit the Highlands
of Scotland, the
Lake District, the
Grand Canyon or the
Great Barrier Reef –
stunning locations are
a real inspiration.*

We are what we
repeatedly do.
Excellence,
therefore, is not an
act, but a habit.

Aristotle

There is a transcendent power in example. We reform others unconsciously when we walk uprightly.

Anne Sophie Swetchine

You see things and
say 'Why?', but I
dream things that
never were; and I
say 'Why not?'

George Bernard Shaw

IN THE MIDDLE OF DIFFICULTY LIES OPPORTUNITY.

Albert Einstein

If you have built
castles in the air, your
work need not be lost;
that is where they
should be. Now put
the foundations
under them.

Henry David Thoreau

The power of
imagination
makes us infinite.

John Muir

Learn about a charity that inspires you to do something fantastic while raising money for their support.

Great things are not
done by impulse,
but by a series of
small things brought
together.

George Eliot

We are all inventors, each sailing out on a voyage of discovery, guided each by a private chart, of which there is no duplicate.

Ralph Waldo Emerson

What we truly and earnestly aspire to be, that in some sense we are.

Anna Jameson

Go confidently in
the direction of your
dreams. Live the life
you have imagined.

Henry David Thoreau

OPTIMISM IS THE FAITH THAT LEADS TO ACHIEVEMENT. NOTHING CAN BE DONE WITHOUT HOPE AND CONFIDENCE.

Helen Keller

He is able who thinks he is able.

Siddhārtha Gautama Buddha

Sit quietly in a forest
or at the edge of the sea
and let natural beauty
fill you with wonder.

Without inspiration the best powers of the mind remain dormant, there is a fuel in us which needs to be ignited with sparks.

Johann Gottfried von Herder

Nothing is impossible
to a willing heart.

John Heywood

Your imagination is
your preview of life's
coming attractions.

Albert Einstein

*Experience a talk
or workshop run
by someone who is
passionate about what
they do.*

Destiny is no matter of chance. It is a matter of choice. It is not a thing to be waited for, it is a thing to be achieved.

William Jennings Bryan

To accomplish great things, we must not only act, but also dream; not only plan, but also believe.

Anatole France